PASTOR C. MARCEL WIGGINS

MONTH OF
HIDDEN TREASURES FOR YOUR SOUL
MANNA
30 DAY DEVOTIONAL

Month of Manna 30 Day Devotional
Hidden Treasures for Your Soul

Copyright © 2022 C. Marcel Wiggins

All rights reserved. No part of this publication may be reproduced, distributed or transmitted in any form or by any means, without prior written permission. Unless otherwise identified, scripture quotations are from the King James Version of the Bible.

Published by
Dreamer Reign, LLC
P.O. Box 291354
Port Orange, FL 32129

www.dreamerreign.com

For Worldwide Distribution
Printed in the U.S.A.

ISBN: 9781952253195
Library of Congress Control Number: 2022943814

Cover Design: C. Marcel Wiggins

DEDICATION

I dedicated this project to the Lord, and His people!

— To my beautiful wife Sanyu, I love you.

— To my sons Joshua and Caleb, I love you both.

— To my mom (Carletta) thank you for all your love and care.

— To Carleshia, LaTisha, Keith, and Shon, I love you.

— To Drs. Roy and EShawnna Smith. I appreciate and love you both.

INTRODUCTION

One thing that is so simple, yet so effective, is encouraging someone. Encouraging phrases such as, "you got this" and "God has you on His mind" can go a long way—more than we know and think. It has been said that, "the body will achieve what the mind believes." So then, belief is connected to behavior. Now, because we know that belief starts in the mind, we can conclude that encourgement can lead to positive behavior.

Romans 10:17 says, "…faith comes by hearing." May your faith in God increase exponentially in the next thirty days. After thirty days, I pray that you keep the cycle of encouragement going by encouraging others. You may be surprised by the responses you get from them—in a good way of course.

The encouragement that fills these pages was first written for my Apostle, Dr. Roy Etienne Smith; he encouraged me to put it in book form to encourage others. It is my prayer that it encourages you as well.

MONTH OF MANNA

Day 1 of 30

—

THANK GOD FOR
RESTORATION

Our God has not changed. He still hastens to perform His Word. He is doing what He said He would in the lives of His people—and your life is no exception. He can and He will bring RESTORATION.

"And I will restore to you the years that the locust hath eaten, the cankerworm, and the caterpillar, and the palmerworm, My great army which I sent among you."

Joel 2:25

MONTH OF MANNA

Day 2 of 30

—

THANK GOD FOR YOUR

FRUSTRATION

Eagles have such a profound way of teaching their eaglets to start hunting for themselves. This is accomplished by food deprivation. That seems cruel at first, but it is a vital part of the learning process. Once the eaglets are hungry and frustrated enough, they will fly to the hunting grounds looking for food.

Frustration is not always negative; it is also positive. God uses it to get His people to take a leap of faith.

"…they shall mount up with wings as eagles; they shall run, and not be weary; and they shall walk, and not faint."

Isaiah 40:31

MONTH OF MANNA

Day 3 of 30

—

THANK GOD FOR YOUR
DIVINE HEALTH

I decree and declare great health over your life in the name of Jesus! You will live a long, full, and healthy life!

"Dear friend, I pray that you may enjoy good health and that all may go well with you, even as your soul is getting along well."

3 John 2:1 (NIV)

"I shall not die, but live, and declare the works of the Lord."

Psalm 118:17

MONTH OF MANNA

Day 4 of 30

—

THANK GOD FOR YOUR
MIRACLE

Your miracle is one decision away. What will you choose? Will you choose to use your faith to receive your miracle?

"When Jesus saw him lie, and knew that he had been now a long time in that case, he saith unto him, Wilt thou be made whole?"

John 5:6

MONTH OF MANNA

Day 5 of 30

—

THANK GOD FOR YOUR
AUTHORITY

The enemy needs you to remain oblivious to your God-given authority. Recognizing and exercising such power only means devastation to his plans. You are a powerful person! Exercise your authority!

"And hath made us kings and priests unto God and His Father; to Him be glory and dominion for ever and ever. Amen"

Revelation 1:6

MONTH OF MANNA

Day 6 of 30

—

THANK GOD FOR YOUR
PROTECTION

Protect - keep safe from harm or injury.

When you feel as though you are alone and unprotected, always know that God is watching over you to help and protect you. There are things the He allows. However, those things can actually help you at the end instead of harming you.

"The Lord of hosts is with us; The God of Jacob is our tronghold [our refuge, our high tower]. Selah."

Psalm 46:7 (AMP)

MONTH OF MANNA

Day 7 of 30

THANK GOD FOR YOUR
VICTORY

HIDDEN TREASURES FOR YOUR SOUL

Victory - a success or triumph over an enemy in battle or war.

In every battle, there are casualties. In every battle, there is a victor and a loser. In every battle, the victor spoils and the loser gets spoiled. In "this battle," you can look forward to the spoils of the enemy because God is fighting with and for you.

"For the LORD your God is He that goeth with you, to fight for you against your enemies, to save you."

Deuteronomy 20:4

MONTH OF MANNA

Day 8 of 30

THANK GOD FOR YOUR
ABUNDANCE

Our God is the God of more than enough. Stop believing Him for just enough. Believe Him for more than enough. He will exceed your expectations.

"The Lord shall open unto thee His good treasure, the heaven to give the rain unto thy land in his season, and to bless all the work of thine hand: and thou shalt lend unto many nations, and thou shalt not borrow."

Deuteronomy 28:12

MONTH OF MANNA

Day 9 of 30

—

THANK GOD FOR YOUR
TIME OF REST

David was a victorious man of war who fought plenty of enemies during his lifetime. After his death, his son Solomon took the throne. Then there was a shift in the kingdom. Although David spent years fighting against surrounding nations, Solomon and the nation of Israel entered into a season of rest. God gave them rest on every side. May God's rest permeate your life.

"But now the LORD my God hath given me rest on every side, so that there is neither adversary nor evil occurrent."

I Kings 5:4

MONTH OF MANNA

Day 10 of 30

—

THANK GOD FOR
SUSTAINING YOU

HIDDEN TREASURES FOR YOUR SOUL

You can change the tonal sound of a piano by using any of the three pedals located at the bottom. The most commonly used pedal is the sustain pedal. It causes the sound to be heard for a longer period of time. This pedal can be used to create smooth transitions from note to note, chord to chord, and section to section. God sustained Elijah by sending him to the house of a widow after the brook dried up. God will sustain you, and keep you throughout every season; trust Him.

"Arise, get thee to Zarephath, which belongeth to Zidon, and dwell there: behold, I have commanded a widow woman there to sustain thee."

I Kings 17:9

MONTH OF MANNA

Day 11 of 30

—

THANK GOD FOR YOUR
INCREASE

When the time is right, and you are ready for it, increase will break out all around you. Until then, continue to have faith because God's timing is impeccable.

"But seek ye first the kingdom of God, and His righteousness; and all these things shall be added unto you."

Matthew 6:33

MONTH OF MANNA

Day 12 of 30

—

THANK GOD FOR YOUR
LEGACY

Live boldly, and make an impact right where you are. Leave a memorable imprint in the hearts of many. Remember: Your legacy will outlive you.

"A good man leaveth an inheritance to his children's children..."

Proverbs 13:22

MONTH OF MANNA

Day 13 of 30

—

GOD IS INTO
YOU

There are numerous signs that indicate a man's interest in a woman. Some of these signs are: making time for her, communicating how he feels about her, and going out of his way to do things for her. God is the same towards you. He makes time for you. He tells you how much He loves you, and goes out of His way to have a relationship with you. Remember, He proclaimed His love for you by dying on the cross.

"For God so loved the world, that He gave his only begotten Son, that whosoever believeth in Him should not perish, but have everlasting life."

John 3:16

MONTH OF MANNA

Day 14 of 30

—

THANK GOD FOR YOUR
WAY OUT

No matter what you go through, there is always a way out. Even when it seems like every door is blocked and locked, there's always an unlocked door you can get to and go through.

"There hath no temptation taken you but such as is common to man: but God is faithful, Who will not suffer you to be tempted above that ye are able; but will with the temptation also make a way to escape, that ye may be able to bear it."

I Corinthians 10:13

MONTH OF MANNA

Day 15 of 30

—

THANK GOD FOR YOUR
REWARD

Sometimes we need to be reminded that nothing we do will go to waste. God has a goal in mind for you. Keep working! Keep walking! Keep winning!

"Be ye strong therefore, and let not your hands be weak: for your work shall be rewarded."

II Chronicles 15:7

Day 16 of 30

—

THANK GOD FOR THE
IMPOSSIBLE

What appears to be impossible, now becomes possible with a Word from God. His Word possesses the power to cause manifestation.

"Now when he had left speaking, he said unto Simon, Launch out into the deep, and let down your nets for a draught. And Simon answering said unto Him, Master, we have toiled all the night, and have taken nothing: nevertheless at Thy Word I will let down the net."

Luke 5:4-5

MONTH OF MANNA

Day 17 of 30

—

THANK GOD FOR YOUR
FAITH JOURNEY

Abraham was not privy to all the details when he decided to follow God, but he knew his faith was taking him somewhere spectacular. Every step of faith you take with God, is another step closer to something spectacular.

"For we walk by faith, not by sight."

II Corinthians 5:7

Day 18 of 30

THANK GOD FOR
HEARING YOU

Do not think for one microsecond that God is deaf or He is ignoring you. He hears you, even when you don't know how to verbalize your prayers. He hears the words of your heart. Keep praying!

"Behold, the LORD'S hand is not shortened, that it cannot save; neither His ear heavy, that it cannot hear:"

Isaiah 59:1

MONTH OF MANNA

Day 19 of 30

—

THANK GOD FOR HIS
PROMISES

HIDDEN TREASURES FOR YOUR SOUL

According to the scriptures, God watches over His Word to perform it. Therefore, you can have unshakeable confidence in Him, knowing what He said will come to pass.

"Then the Lord said to me, "You have seen well, for I am [actively] watching over My Word to fulfill it."

Jeremiah 1:12 (AMP)

MONTH OF MANNA

Day 20 of 30

—

THANK GOD FOR YOUR
STRENGTH

HIDDEN TREASURES FOR YOUR SOUL

May Jehovah-Chatsahi (The Lord my Strength) strengthen your spirit, body, emotions, mind, heart, finances, business ventures, family bonds, relationships, faith, talents, and gifts in Jesus' name.

"It is God that girdeth me with strength, and maketh my way perfect."

Psalm 18:32

MONTH OF MANNA

Day 21 of 30

—

THANK GOD FOR HIS
FAITHFULNESS

Despite your short-comings and mistakes, God yet remains committed to you. His love will never fail you. His mercies are new every morning for you. His Word accomplishes His purposes in your life. He will never leave you nor forsake you. He is faithful to you!

"It is of the Lord's mercies that we are not consumed, because His compassions fail not. They are new every morning: great is Thy faithfulness."

Lamentations 3:22-23

MONTH OF MANNA

Day 22 of 30

—

THANK GOD FOR YOUR
SHIFT

HIDDEN TREASURES FOR YOUR SOUL

Shift - a change or transfer from one place, position, direction, person to another.

Embrace the change. Embrace the transfer. Embrace the shift.

"You intended to harm me, but God intended it for good to accomplish what is now being done, the saving of many lives."

Genesis 50:20 (NIV)

MONTH OF MANNA

Day 23 of 30

THANK GOD FOR YOUR
ABUNDANT LIFE

HIDDEN TREASURES FOR YOUR SOUL

Live your life to the fullest. Broaden your horizon with new and exciting experiences; life is too short for you not to live a full life.

"The thief cometh not, but for to steal, and to kill, and to destroy: I am come that they might have life, and that they might have it more abundantly."

John 10:10

Day 24 of 30

—

THANK GOD FOR YOUR
ACCESS

HIDDEN TREASURES FOR YOUR SOUL

May you discern and take full advantage of ALL of the opportunities that God has for YOU!

"That He would grant you, according to the riches of His glory, to be strengthened with might by His Spirit in the inner man;"

Ephesians 3:16

MONTH OF MANNA

Day 25 of 30

—

THANK GOD FOR YOUR
DIVINE PROVIDENCE

May you have favor with all the necessary people who God intends for you to connect with in your region of influence. May you thrive, flourish, and be effective in all that you put your hands to do.

"And I have said, I will bring you up out of the affliction of Egypt unto the land of the Canaanites, and the Hittites, and the Amorites, and the Perizzites, and the Hivites, and the Jebusites, unto a land flowing with milk and honey."

Exodus 3:17

MONTH OF MANNA

Day 26 of 30

—

THANK GOD FOR HIS

INTENTIONS

Everything happens for a reason. God is intentional about what He allows to happen in your life. It all serves a greater purpose. God will get glory from it all!

"The steps of a good man are ordered by the Lord: and He delighteth in his way."

Psalm 37:23

MONTH OF MANNA

Day 27 of 30

THANK GOD FOR WHAT HE HAS
IN STORE FOR YOU

The things God has in store for you are going to blow your mind!

"But as it is written, Eye hath not seen, nor ear heard, neither have entered into the heart of man, the things which God hath prepared for them that love him."

I Corinthians 2:9

Day 28 of 30

—

THANK GOD FOR YOUR
STABILITY

Your stability should not be predicated upon the conditions of where you are; conditions change. Your sense of security and stability should be rooted and grounded in God.

"I have set the Lord always before me: because He is at my right hand, I shall not be moved."

Psalm 16:8

Day 29 of 30

YOU CAN
DO IT!

When you constantly look to the left and to the right, your eyes can become more focused on what God put in the hands of another rather than on what He has put in yours. You have everything you need to get the job done. You can do it!

"I can do all things through Christ who strengthens me."

Philippians 4:13 (NKJV)

MONTH OF MANNA

Day 30 of 30

—

THANK GOD FOR YOUR
FRESH WIND

May the Spirit of God breathe a fresh wind that revives, rejuvenates, and replenishes you today!

"Then said He unto me, Prophesy unto the wind, prophesy, son of man, and say to the wind, Thus saith the Lord GOD; Come from the four winds, O breath, and breathe upon these slain, that they may live. So I prophesied as He commanded me, and the breath came into them, and they lived, and stood up upon their feet,..."

Ezekiel 37:9-10

CPSIA information can be obtained
at www.ICGtesting.com
Printed in the USA
LVHW060919100323
741170LV00009BA/45